SERENGETI

BY
Lisa Westberg Peters

I would like to thank Bernie Fashingbauer, Director of the Lee and Rose Warner Nature Center, Philip Porter, Professor of Geography, University of Minnesota, David Scheel, University of Minnesota ecologist, and Patricia Anderson for all their help.

CRESTWOOD HOUSE
New York

LIBRARY OF CONGRESS CATALOGING IN PUBLICATION DATA

Peters, Lisa Westberg
  Serengeti / by Lisa Peters

  p. cm. — (National parks)
  Includes index.
  SUMMARY: Describes the history, weather, geography, and natural history of Serengeti National Park and the human activities that take place there.
  1. Natural history—Tanzania—Serengeti National Park—Juvenile literature. 2. Wildlife conservation—Tanzania—Serengeti National Park—Juvenile literature. 3. Serengeti National Park (Tanzania)—Juvenile literature. [1. Serengeti National Park (Tanzania). 2. National parks and reserves—Tanzania.] I. Title. II. Series: National parks
  QH195.T3P47   1989   508.678'27—dc20   89-7859
  ISBN 0-89686-433-2   CIP
                                                                                                                        AC

PHOTO CREDITS

Cover: David Scheel
David Scheel: 4, 10, 12, 15, 18, 19, 21, 23, 24, 25, 26, 30, 31, 32-33, 34, 35, 43, 44
FPG International: (Pastner) 8; (K & G Photo) 13, 14, 16; (Mark Sherman) 28-29; (Scotty Casteel) 39; (Lee Kuhn) 40-41
Susan Reinsborough: 36, 37

Copyright © 1989 by Crestwood House, Macmillan Publishing Company

Macmillan Publishing Company
866 Third Avenue
New York, NY 10022
Collier Macmillan Canada, Inc.

Produced by Carnival Enterprises

Printed in the United States

First Edition

10 9 8 7 6 5 4 3 2 1

TABLE OF CONTENTS

Lions rest in the shade during the day in Serengeti National Park. As the sun goes down, they prepare to hunt.

4

Serengeti National Park

A WILDLIFE SPECTACLE

It is a hot afternoon just south of the equator in East Africa. Several lions sleep on a jumbled pile of rocks. A lizard scampers up to one of the big cats and catches a fly off its face.

For miles around, thousands of animals nibble the sweet green grass of the Serengeti (pronounced Ser-en-GET-ee) plain. Most of them are wildebeest. They look odd with their white beards and curved horns. There are also zebras and sleek gazelles.

Once in a while the grazers look up and check for lions or hyenas. But on this lazy afternoon all seems quiet and safe.

As the sun goes down, the lions begin to stir. A lioness stands on the highest rock to check the plains for a likely meal. But the huge herds have disappeared.

Hours later, two lionesses find a wildebeest that has, for some reason, become separated from the herd. They *stalk* it patiently, but the nervous wildebeest smells lion on the night breeze. The wildebeest runs away in the darkness.

Tonight, the lions fail to catch and kill a meal. They return to their rocks at dawn. Another day on the Serengeti begins.

This is a scene that is played out day after day in Serengeti National Park of Tanzania (pronounced Tan-ze-NEE-a). The scene could have taken place thousands of years ago. In some ways, very little has changed on the Serengeti.

The park's name comes from the African word "siringet," which means endless plain. A woman who lived in the park for years described the plain as "breathtaking and immense, like the sea. It... rolled for mile after mile in a quivering heat haze."

Today Serengeti National Park is the site of the largest gathering of grazing animals in the world. More than two million big game animals live in the park. Vast numbers of smaller creatures live there, too.

The park is also the site of a spectacular, uninterrupted *migration*. Twice a year the wildebeests, zebras, and gazelles migrate from one end of the park to the other.

Humans have watched the Serengeti's splendid wild animals for as long as people have existed. *Fossil* footprints of humanlike creatures have been found near the park. The fossils are almost four million years old.

People are still watching the animals. Today, scientists study them. The Serengeti lions have been studied for more than 20 years.

Tourists watch the animals through camera lenses on photo safaris. Hunting is illegal in the park, but, with licenses, people can hunt elsewhere in the country. *Poachers* watch the animals, too. On the borders of the park, these hunters trap and kill them illegally. But for the most part, the animals of the Serengeti freely roam the plains and woodlands as they always have.

A BULGE IN THE EARTH'S CRUST

A visitor flying over Serengeti National Park will see a huge grassy plain and gently rolling woodlands. Beneath the grass and the trees lies a story billions of years old.

FUN FACT Some Serengeti animals will stand on termite mounds for better views of predators or prey.

The Serengeti rests on top of very old granite. The granite formed almost three billion years ago. Ancient mountains stood here. But all that remains today of the old mountains are hills and rocky outcrops throughout the park. These outcrops are called *kopjes* (pronounced COP-ies).

About 20 million years ago, the Serengeti was covered by lush forests. It was much closer to sea level. But something happened in Africa to make the Serengeti appear as it does today. Forces inside the earth began to push up the earth's crust over East Africa. Scientists are still not sure why.

As East Africa rose, a 5,000-foot *plateau* was created where none had been before. The moist winds from the ocean were now cut off by the highlands. The forests disappeared because it was too dry to support them.

Not only did the crust bulge, it was also pulled apart. The result was long cracks in the crust. In East Africa, one of the cracks is called the Great Rift Valley. Because the crust is thin here, hot melted rock squeezes through. Volcanoes dot the Great Rift Valley. At least one of them is still active.

For millions of years, the wind blew volcanic ash to the Serengeti nearby. The ash settled and created the rolling plain. The grass of the Serengeti thrives on the fertile ash.

One of East Africa's rift valleys may still be splitting, but the movement is slow. If the movement keeps up, the valley may become a seaway like the Red Sea. This change, however, wouldn't happen for millions of years.

HOME OF EARLY HUMANS

Some scientists think these changes in East Africa may have encouraged the *evolution* of humans. They know that ancestors of humans lived in East Africa's forests. As the forests shrank, these early people were forced to look for different food in new places. They wandered onto the grasslands and the *savanna*. Early people might have started looking for roots and seeds. Maybe one of them picked up a stick, a crude tool, to help dig for roots.

On the edge of the Serengeti plain is a 300-foot-deep gorge called Olduvai Gorge.

At some point, millions of years ago, these ancestors began walking upright on two legs instead of on all fours. No one knows exactly why. Nor is anyone sure why some *primates* eventually developed larger brains. But from the evidence found, it is clear these changes first occurred in East Africa.

Water began to collect in the new rift valley that was opening up and formed a string of lakes. One such lake sat on the edge of the Serengeti plain. Early people, or *hominids*, must have settled near this lake.

Years later, the lake dried up. Then a river cut through the layers of volcanic ash like a knife through a layer cake. The river cut a 300-foot-deep gorge, which today is called Olduvai (pronounced OL-doo-vye) Gorge.

8

Mary and Louis Leakey, two English scientists, knew that years of *erosion* had exposed many fossils. In July 1959, Mary Leakey set out to explore a new site. A scrap of bone on the surface caught her eye. She brushed away some nearby dirt and saw two large teeth. She could tell they belonged to the skull of a hominid. The skull was shattered into hundreds of pieces and was nearly two million years old.

Mary Leakey's find that day made everyone realize that East Africa was a very important place in the evolution of humans.

In the late 1970s, Mary Leakey found a trail of fossil footprints near Olduvai. It seemed as if the footprints had been made by two or three hominids, perhaps a man, woman, and child. They had walked upright across a damp ash bed. Later, another layer of ash covered their prints and preserved them. The footprints were three and a half million years old.

The Leakeys continued to explore the area. They found ancient tools and fossils of *extinct* animals. The found fossils of an extinct elephant, a giraffe with antlers, a three-toed horse, hares, rhinos, antelopes, and ostriches. These animals are ancestors of the same creatures that live in the Serengeti today.

EUROPEANS ARRIVE

The Serengeti remained a land of wild animals and primitive people for many centuries. But long ago, people outside of East Africa learned of the area's wildlife riches. For hundreds of years the Chinese, Arabs, and Indians sought Africa's ivory elephant tusks and rhino horns.

In the 1700s, one of Europe's main interests in Africa was the slave trade. Later, European countries were also looking for colonies to settle and for more trading partners. They split up much of Africa among themselves. The land now called Tanzania was put under the "protection" of a German company. Later, the German government took over.

The first travelers who came to East Africa were seeking rhino horns and elephant tusks.

The outsiders brought new diseases to Africa. At the end of the nineteenth century, almost all of the Serengeti's buffaloes and wildebeest died from a disease called rinderpest. It came with the Europeans' cattle.

In the early 1900s, word spread of the Serengeti's lions. Hunters from around the world poured in. They shot lions by the dozen. Sometimes the hunters tied dead zebras to the backs of their vehicles. When lions came to feed on the *carcasses* the hunters shot the lions.

When Germany lost World War I, the British took over Tanzania. It soon became clear to the British that the lions of the Serengeti needed protection. In 1929, the British told hunters they could not shoot lions in a certain area of the Serengeti.

At the same time, a vaccine was developed for rinderpest and was given to cattle. The vaccine helped control the spread of the disease and the number of wildebeest rose again.

The British also set aside a larger area of the Serengeti as a national park in 1940. Since then, the park's boundaries have changed many times.

In the late 1950s, a German zookeeper named Bernhard Grzimek (pronounced ji-mek) arrived in the Serengeti. The British asked him to count the wildlife in the area. They wanted to find out the route of the migrating wildebeest so new park boundaries could be set.

Bernhard and his son, Michael, flew all over the Serengeti plain counting wildebeest. Sometimes they flew only a few hundred feet off the ground.

Before they finished their research, the government set the new park boundaries. Land was added in the north and west. The boundaries closely matched the migration route of the wildebeest.

Today the park has 5,600 square miles. It is about the size of Connecticut. Tanzanians now govern their own country and run the park.

In studying the park, Bernhard Grzimek fell in love with the Serengeti. He wrote a book called *Serengeti Shall Not Die.* It brought the Serengeti's magnificent wildlife to the world's attention.

TROPICAL WEATHER

For most of the year Serengeti National Park is a sunny, dry place. The temperature can climb to 90 degrees Fahrenheit in the afternoon. At night it can drop to 50 degrees. The pleasant temperatures are surprising because the Serengeti is so near the equator. But they can be explained by the park's high elevation.

Twice a year, the rains come. The short rains begin in November and last through December. Heavier, longer rains fall from March through May. The rain comes in violent thunderstorms. Parts of the park become flooded. The roads turn to mud and the rivers that were dry beds most of the year turn into raging torrents.

The climate and terrain of the Serengeti have produced two main types of vegetation here: grasslands and woodlands.

The acacia tree is shaped like an umbrella and is considered a symbol of the African savanna.

The grass plains are in the southeast. They contain different kinds of grasses. Some are cut short by grazing animals and thrive. Others taste like turpentine or are too tough to eat. Another kind is five feet tall.

Acacia (pronounced a-KAY-sha) savanna is in the central area near the settlement of Seronera. The umbrella acacia tree can be found here. The tree is considered a symbol of the African savanna.

The country is more wooded and hilly in the northern and western parts of the park. Yellow-barked acacia trees, or "fever trees," can be found there. They have feathery leaves between long white thorns. Thick forests snake along the river banks.

Different types of animals live in each part of the park. But the vast majority of the Serengeti's mammals migrate back and forth between the woods and the plains. It is this "river" of animals that makes the Serengeti special.

12

On the Serengeti plain, a newborn wildebeest tries to stand up for the first time.

RIVER OF ANIMALS

In November, wet southeast winds from the Indian Ocean blow across the Serengeti plain. Clouds build. Lightning flashes. Thunder shakes the sky.

Huge herds of wildebeest mill in the wooded areas in the northern part of the park. The animals have broad heads like bison. They have tails like horses and long thin legs like antelopes. The Serengeti wildebeest is a type of antelope. But European settlers named it a "wild beast."

When the rain begins to fall on the plain the wildebeest leave the woodlands. One Serengeti warden claimed the animals could see and hear the storms 100 miles to the south. It was the wildebeest's signal to leave and migrate to the plains.

FUN FACT A migrating male wildebeest may claim a territory for as short a time as a few hours.

The wildebeest follow the growth of tender grass shoots. And when the animals leave, they leave in a hurry. They stampede over swollen rivers. Hundreds of wildebeest die and are swept away. Others climb over their bodies to reach the other side. Lions and other meat-eaters, or *predators*, find easy meals when the wildebeest migrate.

When the wildebeest reach the plain, they march in long lines and columns. Well over one million wildebeest migrate at a time.

The wildebeest stay on the plain for the wet season. In January or February, thousands of wildebeest give birth to calves. The calves learn to walk in a few minutes. They must stay near their mothers or be doomed to certain death. Even with the protection of the herd, predators such as hyenas, African hunting dogs, and lions kill many of the young calves.

In May or June, a dry northeast wind begins to blow across the plain. The water holes dry up. The grass turns brown or black if it

Wildebeest have broad heads like bison, tails like horses, and long legs like antelopes.

burns. Even before the grass is gone, the wildebeest gather in huge herds. They line up head to tail in formations that cross the horizon. The wildebeest leave the plains and head north again for the food and water of the woodlands.

In three days, they are gone. Over one year, wildebeest travel a circular route of several hundred miles. Much of their route spills outside the park.

Zebras and Thomson's gazelles migrate, too. There aren't as many of them, but they are also an important source of food for the Serengeti's predators.

Many animals can live together on the plain because they don't compete for the same food. The larger animals eat the longer, tougher grasses. The smaller animals, such as the tiny Thomson's gazelles, eat the shorter green shoots. Today, about two million grazing animals live in the park.

Even though wildebeest calves are guarded by the herd, predators, like this wild dog, still manage to kill many of the calves.

Several lionesses make up the core of a pride. Their job is to find food and raise cubs.

SIMBA

"Simba" is the Swahili word for lion. It's a word that can inspire awe and fear. The Serengeti lion is the reason many people visit the park.

Serengeti lions have been protected for so long that they no longer fear vehicles. They may even lie in the middle of the road and refuse to move for a car. Sometimes they lie in the shade of a researcher's vehicle. In fact, lying around is what lions do most of the time. They spend up to 20 hours a day sleeping or resting.

Lions in the Serengeti are either members of a *pride* or are *nomads*. The core of a pride is several related females: mothers, daughters, sisters, cousins, and aunts. Their main job is to find food and raise cubs.

Males don't always stay with a pride. They may live with more than one pride and travel from one to the other. Their main job is to mark a pride's *territory*, defend it, and mate with the females.

Nomad lions don't belong to a pride. They range far and wide for food. Sometimes nomads are old, weak males or groups of young lions barely old enough to hunt. Pride lions will fiercely defend their territories against nomads. At night, visitors at the lodge in Seronera might hear a lion's loud roar. We think it is a lion's way of saying, "Here I am. Enter my area at your own risk."

Lions don't choose partners for life as some animals do. A male in a pride might mate with all of the females. Lionesses can give birth any time of the year. A lioness ready to give birth will find a spot protected by bushes or high grass for a den. At birth her cubs are covered with dark spots. The spots *camouflage* the cubs and make them harder to see. The cubs stay close to their mother because they need her milk and protection to survive.

By the time the cubs are a few months old, they are too playful to stay hidden in the den. They even try to get a share of the meat from a kill. But cubs are not allowed to eat first. They must compete for their meat.

The life of an adult Serengeti lion is quite good. The lions rarely starve; humans are their only enemies. But life for lion cubs is not as easy.

Cubs will stay with a pride until they are about two years old. Then, very often, the young lions are forced out by hostile adults. They must fend for themselves.

If a pride has to wander far to find *prey*, young cubs may travel along. But it is dangerous for them. They often starve or are killed by predators.

If a new male invades and takes over a pride, he may kill the pride's cubs. Then he mates with the females to produce new offspring. A male will never kill his own cubs or those of a brother.

Serengeti lions prefer the woodlands in the north where prey and water are plentiful. They like to surprise prey from the thickets of a riverbank. The plain has few such hiding places.

FUN FACT A mother lion will keep her tail looped up to rump level and flick it, perhaps to help her cubs keep her in sight in high grass.

Lions eat their prey quickly. If it hasn't eaten for several days, a lion may devour up to 75 pounds of meat at one time.

A pride will mark its territory with urine. Lions from other prides or nomads will know whether the smell is familiar or strange. Sometimes, pride areas overlap. And sometimes a pride will follow the migrating animals.

A 15-year-old lion in the Serengeti is a very old lion. Some lions die from disease. Others are caught by poachers' traps or are shot by hunters outside the park.

But the main event in a lion's life is the hunt for food.

THE HUNT

A pride of lions is hunting late in the day. They spot a sick wildebeest. The lions crouch in the tall grass, moving ahead only when the wildebeest looks away. For half an hour, they stalk it.

Once lions have finished eating their kill, hyenas and vultures finish the meal. No part of the dead animal is wasted.

When one of the lionesses is close enough, she bursts out of the tall grass. She pulls the animal down and bites its neck. The other females rush to join the kill. The wildebeest dies in a few minutes.

When the male lion arrives, he snarls and growls and the females give up the catch. He feeds alone for a while. Three cubs bound over to the carcass. They tear off small chunks of meat.

After a while, the male lets the females join in. The lions snarl and snap at each other. They eat as fast as they can until their bellies are full with meat.

During the night the male guards the carcass against hyenas. The hyenas circle the lions and the kill. They wait for their chance.

Several hours later the male snacks again. At dawn, the lions leave. The hyenas close in to finish off the bones. By this time, vultures roost in the trees nearby. They wait for whatever scraps are left.

At this hunt, the cubs were lucky. The wildebeest was big enough

FUN FACT A male lion's thick mane protects him when he fights another lion.

for all the lions to share. When the prey is smaller, cubs are often left out of the meal.

It's a myth that male lions leave all the hunting to the females. Females do most of the hunting, but males are good hunters, too.

Hunts often fail, but lions are good *scavengers*. They steal kills from hyenas, jackals, and other lions.

When the big herds of prey have moved on, a meal can be hard to find. A lion may go nearly a week without eating. At the next meal, it may eat up to 75 pounds of meat. That's enough to make a lion want to sleep all day.

A LION SCIENTIST

Thousands of people see the Serengeti's lions each year, but only a few people study them.

David is an *ecologist* from the University of Minnesota. He spent a year and a half in the Serengeti studying how the behavior of the prey affects the way lions hunt.

This is how David did his research:

He and another scientist would find a pride of lions and shoot a *tranquilizer* dart into an adult female. They attached a large brown collar with a radio transmitter the size of a tin can onto the female. On the ground, he could follow the radio signal for a few miles. From the air, he could follow it for a longer distance.

David and the other scientist followed lions in two vehicles. They watched them hunt in the nine or ten nights surrounding a full moon. Without the light of the moon, it was too dark to see. The two scientists watched for many things: The size of the herd of prey; how alert they were; how many of the herd were young, old, or sick; whether there were bushes or trees to hide behind; and whether there was more than one type of animal in the herd.

Scientists think grazing animals stay in groups because it is safer. Being part of a group allows each animal to be less watchful because chances are others in the herd will be looking up at any given time. David watched the prey to see how many raised their heads. And he watched the lions to see if that affected the way they hunted.

FUN FACT Lions can make a purring sound, but only when they exhale.

Ecologists put collars with radio transmitters on lions to track their movements in the Serengeti.

When the lions were hunting, David tried not to start the engine of the car. The noise might have made the animals raise their heads.

Sometimes the lions walked all night. Sometimes they slept all night, especially if they were well fed.

David watched 218 lion hunts. Only 30 of those hunts resulted in kills. Altogether, he spent 3,000 hours watching lions.

Scientists in the Serengeti usually live at the Serengeti Wildlife Research Center near Seronera. There is no running water in the concrete block houses. Instead, people have to catch rainwater from the roofs. They store it in big tanks. It is important to have enough water for the dry season.

The Serengeti lion study is one of the longest continuous wildlife projects ever done. Scientists recognize lions by their ear notches, scars, or whisker spot patterns. "Every lion on the plains has been studied and their mothers before them," David says.

LAND OF PREDATORS

The lion is the best-known Serengeti predator. But there are four other important predators in the park.

The spotted hyena is the most abundant one. It looks like a fierce dog, but is actually related to the cat family. The hyena, however, hunts and fights like a dog.

Hyenas prefer to live on the plains in clans. A clan might have up to 100 hyenas in it. The females are the leaders.

Most people think of the hyena as a scavenger. Hyenas do look for vultures circling over a dead animal and feed on the carcass. But the hyena is also a bold hunter at night. Hyenas don't stalk prey the way lions do. They can chase an animal for several miles at about 40 miles per hour. Hyenas cooperate in a hunt. When they catch an animal, they kill it by tearing it to pieces. The method seems cruel to humans, but death comes very quickly. When it is time to eat, though, hyenas fight for their share. They will lead their young to the kill so they can eat, too.

The African hunting dog is a much less common Serengeti predator. Its coat is splotchy with black, white, brown, and yellow patches. It has big, round ears. Hunting dogs can live either on the plain or in open woodlands. They run in packs of 6 to 20 animals. The dogs raise their young in burrows. Up to 16 pups will be born in a litter.

Hunting dogs will often charge into a herd to scatter it. They watch the animals and pick out a slow or sick one. If they find an animal to chase, they can run for long distances.

Like the hyena, the hunting dog kills its prey by tearing it apart. Back at the den, pups will beg for food. The adults will spit up, or *regurgitate*, food for the pups.

Cheetahs are the sprinters of the Serengeti plain. They are the fastest mammals on Earth. They can run 60 miles per hour. They must stalk their prey until they are quite close, however. Cheetahs can't run very far or they will get too hot.

Cheetahs usually hunt alone during the day. Because they run so fast they need to have keen eyesight. They don't defend a territory.

FUN FACT Serengeti predators have one thing in common: They spend about 20 hours a day doing nothing.

Some animals of the Serengeti have been protected for so long that they no longer fear tourists.

Instead, they follow the herds of wildebeest and gazelles. Sometimes a mother cheetah will give a live gazelle fawn to her cub so it can practice hunting. When a cub is one and a half years old, it leaves its mother to hunt alone.

Leopards are perhaps the most mysterious of the predators in the Serengeti. They are hard to see because they rest in the branches of trees. Their dappled coats provide good camouflage.

Leopards hunt alone at night. They are very patient. They like to hide behind bushes and shrubs to sneak up on their prey. They will eat many animals, such as hares, game birds, gazelles, and impalas. A leopard will usually kill its prey with a neck bite. Afterward, it often drags the dead animal up into a tree. By doing this, it hides its meal from hyenas, lions, and vultures.

People often confuse cheetahs and leopards. A cheetah has a black stripe running from the corner of each eye to the corner of its mouth. The cheetah is slighter in build than the leopard. Cheetah and leopard spots are different, too.

Another way to tell the difference is by watching their behavior. Cheetahs can be seen on the plain in the daytime. Leopards probably will be in the woodlands resting on the branches of trees.

LIFE IN THE WOODLANDS

There is a wealth of wildlife in the park's wooded areas. Many of the park's several hundred kinds of birds live in the acacia savanna. Visitors might see storks, ravens, hawks, herons, and vultures.

Spoonbill storks are one of the many kinds of birds that have found niches in the acacia savanna.

The park has six kinds of vultures. Each of them fills a separate *niche* because they eat differently or eat different kinds of meat.

Many antelopes, hares, baboons, and porcupines also live in the savanna. Baboons eat grass, roots, fruit, and insects. They also kill young antelopes. Baboons travel in troops, which can have 30 to 100 members.

Farther north and west, buffaloes graze in the hilly woodlands and thick forests along the rivers. They prefer the shade of the woodlands to the open plain. Lions hunt the buffaloes but this can be dangerous. Buffaloes fight back.

Also in the woodlands is Africa's beautiful antelope, the impala. It is rust colored, with black strips on either side of its white rump patches. The male impala has two long horns.

Giraffes browse on the highest branches of the acacia trees. Hippos wallow in the deep pools of the rivers.

In the woodlands of Serengeti National Park, giraffes eat acacia leaves.

The elephant is a relative newcomer to the park. Pushed south by humans, elephants are now feeding on the trees in the park and are destroying many of them.

The dry Serengeti doesn't seem like crocodile country. But the large reptiles live in a few rivers in the north. Antelopes drinking at the shore must stay alert for the crocodiles' snapping jaws.

The famous African tsetse (pronounced TSET-see) fly also thrives in the woodlands. The tsetse fly of the Serengeti does not carry a deadly disease, as it does elsewhere. But its stinging bite bothers both people and wildlife.

ROCKY ISLANDS

Kopjes poke out of the grassy Serengeti plain. They are just old weathered granite. But for the animals, they are oases.

Often, water collects in cracks and low spots. Animals come to

A lion drinks water that has collected in the cracks of a kopje.

drink from the pools. Trees and shrubs give shade on hot sunny afternoons. Flowers bloom in abundance.

Lions use the kopjes for den sites. The rocks hide the cubs from hyenas and other predators. Poisonous snakes, such as the spitting cobra and the puff adder, also hide in the rocks.

A small furry animal called the hyrax is often found in the kopjes. One kind of hyrax eats the grass around the base of the rocks. Another kind climbs the rocks and eats the leaves of the acacias.

Birds nest in the trees on a kopje. Small antelopes and mongooses are often seen near the rocks. The kopjes may look like barren islands, but they teem with plant and animal life.

PREDATOR AND PREY TOGETHER

Tourists might think the Serengeti's gazelles are swift and graceful just for their benefit. Running gazelles make great pictures to bring home. The truth is that pressure from predators has made the grazing animals the way they are. Slowly, over millions of years, the Serengeti's grazing animals developed many ways to escape predators.

The Serengeti antelopes are speedy. It is often their only defense against lions. Over time the swiftest antelopes survive to produce young, while the slow, sick, or old animals fall to the predators.

The Serengeti's grazing animals also have bulging eyes. This gives them wide-angle vision. They have a better chance of seeing predators.

The coats of the prey are often beige or brown. This should be good camouflage except that plains animals graze in large herds. Animals in large groups are more easily spotted than single animals. On the open plain, however, there is safety in numbers. Many eyes and many noses are more likely to detect a predator.

Animals that live alone prefer the woodlands. They can hide in shrubs. A herd cannot do that.

The wildebeest have adjusted to the pressures of predators. When they migrate, they often walk in single file. It reduces the chance of stumbling on a lion.

On the wide Serengeti plain, animals stay together. Many eyes and ears are more likely to detect a predator.

Most wildebeest calves are born at the same time of year. This amounts to tens of thousands of calves. There are so many calves that predators can't possibly eat them all. Therefore, many calves reach adulthood.

The animals of the Serengeti have learned how to escape from predators. Gazelle fawns stay very still in the grass, hoping to be invisible. Adult gazelles hop away in great zigzags. This confuses a predator that is trying to focus on one animal.

Animals also have developed weapons. Giraffes kick with powerful legs. Zebras kick and bite. Buffaloes can gore with their horns.

Predators have adapted to their environment, too. Lions are slow, but their strength, sharp teeth, and claws work well for them. Chee-

So many wildebeest calves are born at the same time of the year that predators can't possibly eat them all. That's why many calves reach adulthood.

This cheetah is wearing a collar with a radio transmitter. While the cheetah tracks the wildebeest, scientists track it.

tahs are small and can't take down large prey. But they are fast enough to outrun the speedy gazelles.

Leopards have learned that patience pays. A stalk might take hours, but a meal at the end is worth the wait.

Lions and other predators remove only a small part of the herds every year. Rainfall and the supply of food also affect the size of the animal population.

Visitors might be shocked to see a lion kill a delicate gazelle. People feel sorry for the gazelle. But predators are just part of life and death in the Serengeti. A lion eats a gazelle. Hyenas feed on the remaining scraps. A vulture feeds, too. The insects move in and remove all traces of the kill.

FUN FACT In the Serengeti, an average of one hunt in five by predators is successful.

The animals of the Serengeti have learned how to escape from predators. They hide in the tall grass or run in zigzags.

In the dry season, the Serengeti is often scorched black by man-made and natural fires.

FUEL FOR FIRE

The Serengeti plain has a split personality. In the growing season from November to May, the plain is green from the rains. In the dry season, it is often scorched black by fire.

There are many reasons for the fires. Poachers start fires because burning off the old grass stimulates new grass growth. Poachers hope the new grass will attract the herds of game to their area. Africans may burn grass outside the park to encourage new growth for their cattle. Some of the fires spread to the park. Sometimes they will set a fire after they steal someone's cattle. The fire covers their tracks.

To combat the illegal or accidental fires, park officials set controlled fires. Patches of grassland are burned. The fires are set at a time when they will do the least damage.

Sometimes vultures and other birds will gather at the front of a fire to catch the insects and small animals that are running from the heat and flames.

Birds will often collect at the fire front. They eat the insects, lizards, snakes, and mice fleeing from the heat.

Fire makes it hard for young trees in the park's woodlands to grow. Scientists are now studying the effects of fire on the woodlands.

THE PROUD MASAI

Humans and their ancestors have roamed the Serengeti for millions of years. The most recent residents are the *Masai* people.

The Masai still live in the Great Rift Valley of East Africa. It is thought that they migrated from North Africa hundreds of years ago. They were cattle herders then. They still are.

FUN FACT The Masai don't count the cattle in their herds. Knowing the exact number of animals is considered bad luck.

The Masai have always been known as proud, fierce warriors. Other African tribes feared them. Their warlike nature kept away slave traders. But when Europeans settled in Africa, the Masai lost much of their land. Disease nearly wiped out their cattle. Many of their people died.

Today, the Masai live in small settlements outside the park. The women build rounded houses, called *bomas*, from frames of sticks. They pack grass all around. Then they smear cattle dung on the outsides. It dries to a hard crust.

The houses are arranged in a big circle. A fence made of thorn bushes surrounds the houses. At night the Masai herd their cattle into the enclosure. This protects them from lions and leopards.

The Masai love their children. They have an expression: "May God give you children. May God give you cattle."

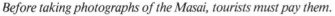

Before taking photographs of the Masai, tourists must pay them.

Cattle are a symbol of wealth for the Masai. They rarely butcher them. The tribe's diet is mostly milk, plants, and herbs. Once in a while, they will eat a goat or cow.

The Masai also drink cattle blood. It is an important part of their traditional diet. They puncture a vein in the cow to get it. They are careful not to kill the cow. The Masai believe the blood gives them strength.

The Masai think all of the world's cattle belong to them. They still raid other tribes and steal cattle. The Masai say they are simply getting back what is theirs.

A Masai warrior is easily recognized. He paints his body and his hair with red clay. Then he draws patterns in the paint. He lets his hair grow long and adorns it with ostrich feathers. The Masai also pierce their earlobes. The hole in the ear is gradually enlarged until it

The Masai live in small settlements outside of Serengeti National Park.

hangs like a big hoop earring. Then it is decorated with beads.

A Masai tribesman, Ole Saitoti, has written books about his people. "I may sound pessimistic," he writes, "but I have reason to be. The Masai are a people whose time has passed." He says the Masai must have education and land to survive.

SAFARI!

Pat and Bernie have visited East Africa and Serengeti National Park on photo safaris several times. With each trip they see more of Africa's beauty. Although they usually travel in February, they take along plenty of summer clothes. They also bring light jackets or sweaters for the cooler evenings. To keep out dust, they pack their cameras and other items in plastic bags.

Pat brings plenty of film. She took 2,000 slides on one trip. Some people bring 50 to 75 rolls of film, Bernie says.

Travelers to East Africa must have current passports, visas, and several shots including tetanus, cholera, and yellow fever. They also must take pills for malaria.

Their flight leaves the United States and lands first in a European city, such as Amsterdam or Rome. Then the flight continues to Nairobi, Kenya.

From there, Pat and Bernie's tour group boards vans. Their group visits many game reserves and parks in both Kenya and Tanzania.

The road to the Serengeti is a rough, two-track dirt road. Pat says, "You go from pothole to pothole." It takes a long time to get anywhere in East Africa because of the roads, she says.

Pat and Bernie's group stays at the lodge at Seronera. Most tourists stay there or at the lodge at Lobo, farther north. The lodge is beautiful. It is built around a huge kopje. To conserve energy and water, the lodge cuts off electrical and water service for a part of each day.

But tourists don't come to the Serengeti for the lodgings. They come to see the animals. A typical day includes a game run early in the morning and a second one late in the afternoon. In the Serengeti "you can see more wildlife in half an hour than you'd see in the rest of the world for a month," Bernie says.

During a safari, guides take tourists on game runs where the tourists can photograph animals found in the Serengeti and surrounding areas.

Pat agrees. "There are over a million wildebeest in the Serengeti, and the first time we went, I'm sure we saw them all."

Tourists most want to see the lions. Bernie says there are plenty. "It's no trick to see lions." In fact, the sleepy cats will often lie on the road and not move for the van.

"You could drive over a lion," Pat says. "You've never been ignored until you've been ignored by a lion."

Neither Pat nor Bernie has seen a lion kill take place. They've seen lions stalk their prey. But a stalk can go on for hours and many times is unsuccessful.

On one trip, they saw a pack of African hunting dogs near their den. "They look itchy, like old farm dogs that have been abused," Pat says.

The acacia grasslands of Tanzania draw thousands of tourists each year.

But wild dogs are good parents, she says. She saw them spit up food from an earlier kill for their young pups at the den.

Tourists will see members of the Masai tribe when they visit East Africa. The Masai require tourists to pay for taking their photographs. Pat said her driver urged them to pay for fear the Masai would slash his tires with their spears.

Pat and Bernie's African trips are about three weeks long, but their memories last a lifetime.

THE SLAUGHTER IN AFRICA

It is against the law to shoot animals in Serengeti National Park and other African parks. Next door, the country of Kenya allows no hunting anywhere. But all over Africa, people are killing the animals anyway. Here's why.

A small number of animals are killed by Africans to feed their families. Many Africans are poor, and it doesn't cost them anything to kill game for a meal.

But that is not how most of Africa's animals are dying. For hundreds of years, people around the world have paid Africans to kill elephants for the ivory tusks. They have paid Africans to kill rhinos for the horns.

The ivory tusks are made into jewelry and candlesticks. The tusks were widely used for piano keys. A rhino's horn is not made of rare materials. It is made of a substance that is also found in hair and fingernails. But the Chinese consider the horns very valuable. They use them for many types of medicines. Arabs in the country of North Yemen also want rhino horns. They carve them into handles for daggers. Rhino horns sell for thousands of dollars. Today, because of all the hunting, rhinos face extinction.

People also kill wildebeest and use their tails for fly whisks. They kill leopards for their coats. They capture many kinds of live animals for exotic pets. For example, whole flocks of Fisher's lovebirds have been caught in nets inside the park by poachers.

In most cases, the demand for Africa's animals comes from people outside of Africa.

Every day, rangers capture poachers who are illegally hunting the Serengeti's wild animals.

Some poachers are using automatic rifles to kill animals. They use two-way radios. They haul away the carcasses in trucks. The park patrols its borders constantly for poachers. Sometimes poachers shoot and kill rangers. Many poachers are caught and arrested, but it is demand that keeps poaching alive.

DISAPPEARING ANIMALS

In 1930, the British rulers of the country now known as Tanzania faced a dilemma. Some colonists wanted to save the wild animals at the expense of developing the country. Others wanted to stop protecting the animals.

The British rulers couldn't agree with either side. They decided that

43

The wild animals of the Serengeti plain are protected within the boundaries of Serengeti National Park.

the "march of civilization" must go on. But the animals should be protected "for all time" in game reserves and parks.

More than 50 years later, that is what has happened. Africa used to be islands of people surrounded by a sea of wildlife. Today it is becoming islands of animals surrounded by people.

Serengeti National Park is one of those islands. Its animals are safe only if people protect them. Poaching removes many animals. A growing African population crowds them. More and more people need places to live, to farm, and to graze cattle. Some Africans don't feel a need to protect the animals. African farmers have as little fondness for baboons as American ranchers have for coyotes.

American settlers, in their march to civilize our country, nearly killed off the bison. The same thing is happening to Africa's animals.

Tourists could bring hope for the animals. If Africans earn more money from tourism than from poaching, the animals will benefit. Hope comes from education, too. People who understand animals are more likely to protect them.

For now, the great herds of animals still thunder across the Serengeti plain as they have for centuries. It is a scene from the past. If people are careful, it will be a vision of the future.

FOR MORE PARK INFORMATION

For more information about Serengeti National Park, call a travel agent for photo safari information or write to:

National Park Headquarters
P.O. Box 3134
Arusha, Tanzania

PARK MAP

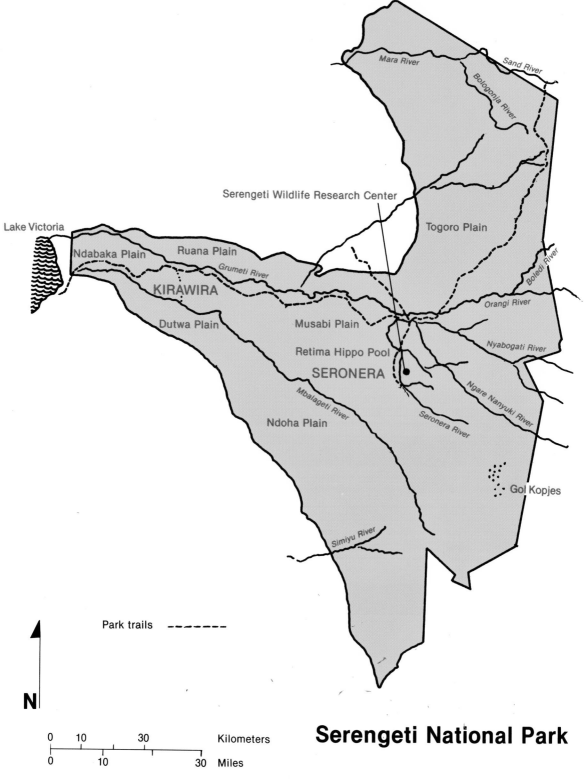

Lake Victoria

Serengeti Wildlife Research Center

Mara River

Sand River

Bologonia River

Togoro Plain

Ndabaka Plain

Ruana Plain

Grumeti River

Boledi River

KIRAWIRA

Orangi River

Dutwa Plain

Musabi Plain

Nyabogati River

Retima Hippo Pool

SERONERA

Mbalageti River

Seronera River

Ngare Nanyuki River

Ndoha Plain

Gol Kopjes

Simiyu River

Park trails

N

| 0 | 10 | 30 | Kilometers |
| 0 | 10 | 30 | Miles |

Serengeti National Park

GLOSSARY / INDEX

GLOSSARY / INDEX

DATE			